MONSTERS
OF THE
IMAGINATION

Amazing Creature Designs by Global Artists

Dopress Books

CYPI PRESS

Contents

Chapter 1: Digital Painting

Chapter 2: Traditional Hand Drawing

Chapter 3: 3D Modeling & Rendering

Chapter 4: Sculpture

Chapter 1
Digital Painting

Yerbol Bulentayev

Materials and tools
Wacom Intuos 5, Adobe Photoshop
Artist website
eksrey.artstation.com

Bulentayev's subject matter is monsters, whether it's creatures from other planets or fantasy characters. The challenge is to see beyond the distraction of the conspicuous to capture its unique self. Bulentayev's goal is to inspire those who see his works to look more carefully at the world around them, to discover beauty in unusual things and to expand their imagination.

When did you start designing monsters?

I have been designing monsters ever since I started drawing; the main reason is I like to draw monsters.

Monster design is a highly imaginative work. Where do you usually find inspiration?

I get inspiration everywhere, in movies or from TV shows, but mostly I get it from the internet.

1 2

1
Zombie-Superman
It is a rough daily sketch. I wanted to make the superman less handsome.

2
TROG
Illustration for card game "Cry Havoc." I followed some descriptions of what should be on the picture.

1
Max Vader
This artwork was made for the cgplus.com contest.

2
Warrior 1

What tools and materials do you prefer? What are their features and how do they help you with your work?

I'm using Adobe Photoshop and Wacom Intous; sometimes I like to draw on paper. I like Photoshop because it works very well and there are few errors.

Which monster design, either from a movie or a game, is your favorite and why? How did the design inspire you?

My favorite monster is from "The Guyver" movie; there are very cool monsters, and I have liked them since my childhood.

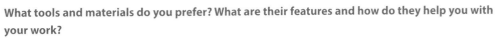

1

1
The Alian in the Desert
It's a concept sketch. I wanted to create
some extraterrestrial weapons.

Ivan Laliashvili

Materials and tools
Photoshop CS6, Zbrush, 3D Max, 3D Coat, KeyShot
Artist website
http://ivanlaliashvili.deviantart.com/
https://www.artstation.com/artist/laliashvili

Ivan Laliashvili is a concept artist and illustrator who studied at the Academy of Fine Arts in Saint Petersburg, Russia. Ivan is currently working as an artist in the video game industry.

When did you start designing monsters?

I have loved monsters, especially dragons, all of my life. I think it's fun to create fantasy creatures that are very strong, wild and powerful but at the same time really wise and smart.

1 | 2

1
Golem

2
Apophis

1 | 2 | 1
1 | 3 | Ammit

2
Vodyanoy

3
Dragon

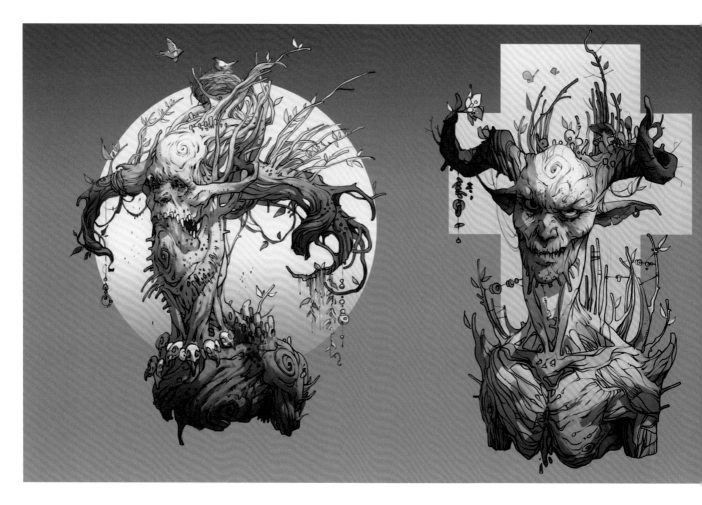

Monster design takes a lot of imagination. Where do you usually find inspiration?

I generally find inspiration from great animations or movies. For me it is the best inspiration.

What tools and materials do you prefer? What are their features and how do they help you with your work?

I prefer classical and traditional methods of drawing. But a couple of times I tried using 3D programs, and I like experimenting with them, too.

1		1	2	3
2	3	Ents	Swamp Creatures	Swamp Creatures

What is your favorite monster design from a movie or game? What inspired you from the design?

My favorite monster design is from "The Lord of the Rings" films and Guillermo del Toros'"Pacific Rim. "The animated monsters look amazing. They resemble real-life creatures with different characteristics and behaviors. I love them because they are so huge and big.

How do you gather materials in your daily life and apply them to your works?

Thank you for this question. I think this is the most important thing in our professional art career. Every day and night, we should copy, collect and memorize different art and visual materials from books, the internet and of course the real life. I take screenshots from games and movies, and save illustrations and concept art forms from other awesome artists. When I travel, I take photos so I can use them for inspiration in the future.

1	
1	2

1
Forest Guardians (details)

2
Forest Guardians

Nicotine

Materials and tools
Photoshop
Artist website
https://www.artstation.com/artist/nicotine

Nicotine is a senior concept designer, signed artist of Games Workshop and art consultant of NetEase Games. He is the founder and CEO of DRock-Art in Hangzhou, China, and is currently developing the original sci-fi project "Boundary Apocalypse." He has participated in the development of international games such as "Darksiders II," "Warhammer 40K," "The Elder Scrolls," "The Tower of Eternity," just to name a few. His works have been recommended on the cover of "CGHUB" several times and recorded in the "Editor Picks Archive." In 2015, he designed the cover of the "Black Library- Warhammer" and his works were featured on "Fantasy Art," "HXSD Special Interview" and "CG Artists Alliance Yearbook".

Where do you usually find inspiration?

I am usually inspired by a kind of fossil or specimen. Of course, the excellent concepts of a certain movie or game can also influence me. Most of the time, drawing monsters is another way for me to enjoy my time.

1	2

1
Marginal Revelation - Abyss Monster - Erfan Sosa
As early as the Throne Empire, it was recorded in the chronicle that the creatures were living in the hot volcano cave of the Paronamile plateau of throne star. They live on organic and metallic ore in the magma. The magic will only be called out during major battles. His hammer, the Hellbreaker Hagan, has been integrated into his body, and is his most powerful weapon. It always leaves the enemy terrified.

2
Marginal Apocalypse - the Interstellar Vatican – Dark Execution Man
Dark Execution Man can easily distinguish the individual objects that need to be punished. The special armed forces also made the creativity of the interstellar Vatican engineers steady and developed.

Which artists and art forms have influenced you the most?

H • R • Giger, and Cthulhu in his work "Warhammer 40K."

What tools and materials do you prefer? What are their features and how do they help you with your work?

I mainly use computer graphics softwares. It can express the conceptual idea effectively and is convenient for reshaping and revising.

What are the features of your work? How do you find your style?

My works are mostly dark and chaotic. I am good at using my imagination in concept design on objects such as machines and creatures. I will usually listen to music with a strong sense of rhythm when I am working. It inspires me a lot.

| 1 | 2 |

1
Marginal Apocalypse - Interstellar Vatican - Blind Laugher Legion Warrior
These were the warriors of the interstellar Vatican, and their eyes were given to annihilation. At that moment they also received the eyes of the Unifonso.

2
Marginal Apocalypse - Abyss Heir - Sasol's Attendants
This is also the monster in the marginal apocalypse. The ratio of the monster in animation is smaller. He has multiple heads, a flesh shield on his right arm, and an exposed skeleton structure. All of these qualities highlight the horror of the monster.

1

2 | 3

1

Marginal Apocalypse - Abyss Heir - Gigantic Tyrant

This monster is famous for its giant arms and brutal and sadistic character. Its armor is made of huge stones that are able to channel high-energy radioactive elements. This allows its armor to grow wildly and repair easily when injured.

2

Marginal Apocalypse - Abyss Heir - Acne Control

The manic monster has the ability to frustrate its enemies. His armor gives off an extremely harsh odor that can affect the enemy's judgment. Its left hand is a particle gun with a giant blade, and its right arm is used to spread a dark sore virus, known as the giant scepter.

3

Marginal Apocalypse - Bad Wrist Cleaning Event

The bad wrist cleaning event is the beginning of the abyssal beasts invading the universe. This ignorant beast — Evil Wrist — inadvertently intruded into the real universe, and then began its greedy, engulfing journey.

Step 01: the original line sketches

Step 02: highlight the focus with different shades of gray

Step 03: the final work

Sarita Kolhatkar

Materials and tools
Adobe Photoshop
Artist website
http://www.BubbleRockets.com

Sarita Kolhatkar is a professional concept artist and illustrator, working in the gaming and film industry. Sarita earned her BFA in animation and illustration from San José State University in California. Since then, She has built a portfolio of work spanning the last eight years, working for gaming studios internationally (in Seattle, Bangalore, Dubai), as well as locally in Vancouver, Canada. The dreamy and surreal aesthetic of her work is well reflected in the character conceptualization and illustrations.

Where do you usually find inspiration for monster design?

A lot of the inspiration comes from reading old cultural folk tales. Those are the best because they are usually stories that were used to ignite fear within people, so a lot of stories are full of different kinds of monsters.

Which artists or art forms have most influenced your creations?

The filmmaker Tim Burton is, of course, one of my favorites. But I also love the sketchy art style of illustrator Dave McKean, the masterfully dark and gothic puppets from Handsome Devil Puppets, the creature designer Simon Lee and the artist Blake Neubert.

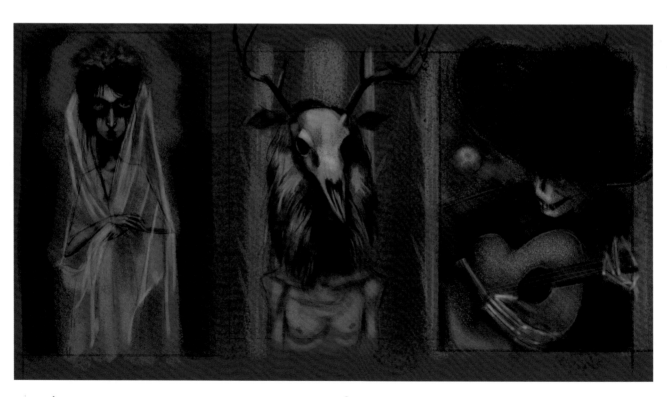

1 | 2

1
Monster Design Color Concepts
After I do a rough sketch of a monster in Adobe Photoshop, I will add a quick and light wash of hues on a neutral gray background to explore the colors and composition.

2
White Crow
Created for the game "Afterland".

1
A ghostly demon, created for the game "Afterland".

2
Created for the game "Afterland".

3
Inspired by an old Brazilian folktale and created for the game "Afterland".

4
Rusulka
Mermaid demon inspired by Russian folklore and created for the game "Afterland".

5
Created for the game "Afterland".

What tools and materials do you prefer? What are their features and how do they help you with your work?

I mostly enjoy working in Adobe Photoshop because I can get out ideas and illustrations quickly and efficiently. I also carry around a sketchbook where I'm always doing concepts and storing ideas to explore later.

1 2
3 4 | 5

1
The Ringleader
Created for the game
"Afterland".

2
Created for the game
"Afterland".

3
Caipora Puppet Demon
Inspired by Brazilian folklore
and created for the game
"Afterland".

4
Misery
Created for the game
"Afterland".

5
Mischief & Misery
Created for the game
"Afterland".

What is your favorite monster design, either from a movie or game? What inspired you?

My favorite monster design is the Caipora Puppet Demon (see image 3) that I did for the game "Afterland" by Imaginary Games. This was inspired by an old Brazilian folk tale. I really like the way the composition turned out, and I love the way the smoke creates a dreaminess around the character.

1
Created for the game "Afterland".

2
Caterpillar from Alice in Wonderland
Created for the game "Afterland".

Pavel Romanov

Materials and tools
Photoshop CS6
Artist website
*https://www.artstation.com/
artist/Cynic*

Pavel Romanov is a freelance 2D artist, illustrator and concept artist. He has worked for the following companies (freelance concept-art illustration): Applibot, Games Workshop, Wargaming. net (2D artist-textures) , PAIZO, HEX Entertainment, Gamecostudios and others.

When did you start designing monsters?

I began painting as a child and then gave up the hobby. Later in life I returned to it. Movies such as "Teenage Mutant Ninja Turtles," "Gremlins," "Star Wars" and "Dracula" inspired me to draw. I later received an education in art. I got a job as a texture artist at Wargaming. net, where I began my career as an artist.

Where do you usually get your inspiration for monster design?

Like many other artists, I find inspiration in movies and books. I like to read art books and play computer games.

Which artists or art forms have had the most influence on you?

The Pre-Raphaelites had a great influence on me. I still admire the color and plots in their paintings. A lot of contemporary artists are interesting, each with their own drawing style.

What tools and materials do you prefer? What are their features and how do they help you with your work?

I only draw in Photoshop. I tried to work in other programs, such as SAI and Painter, but none of them felt as comfortable as Photoshop.

As a concept artist, could you share some of your important experiences?

Drawing is a lifestyle; it's an interesting hobby as well as work. To create a good painting, you need to work hard, but all of this work also needs to be fun. The very process of learning is very exciting, and there is no end to it. The artist learns all of his life.

1 | 2

1
Evil Bull
Created for card game "Leap of Faith".

2
Goblin

In a movie or a game, which monster design is your favorite and why? How did they inspire you about the design?

It's hard to single out a specific film. I like many. Among the most beloved genres are horror films and historical ones. Recently, I began watching TV shows. One of the best in my opinion is "Games of Thrones" and "The Walking Dead."

What are the unique features of your work? How did you find your style?

Initially, I tried to imitate many artists. I saw interesting elements in other people's styles. In the end, I somehow formed my own style. I try to continue to bring something new, and change up my style.

1 | 2 3

1
SHAN-TI
Created for card game "Star Crusade".

2
King Dragon (advanced)

3
King Dragon (regular)

Thiago Almeida

Materials and tools
Photoshop
Artist website
www.behance.net/thiagoalmeida

Thiago Almeida is an illustrator and freelance artist. He works on concepts for games, mobile game, movies and advertisements. He is passionate about drawing, movies and games, and spends a lot of time drawing and studying. Thiago loves sketching on his sketchbook, where he creates the most unique creatures and characters. Creativity is his best quality.

Where do you usually find inspiration for monster design?

I constantly look for references to help me with my creations. I play many games, and watch a lot of movies and TV series, always observing the costumes and creature design. This helps me when I need to create something new. I search for all of these references in my mind, and look for new visual references and start to scribble. After that, several unique designs appear.

What tools and materials do you prefer to work with? What are their features and how do they help you with your work?

I use Photoshop to make my sketches and finalize my drawings. I also like to scribble in my sketchbook to create new characters, and sometimes I use these sketches as a basis to start my paintings.

1 | 2

1
Demontaur

2
Hamuul Runetotem Fanart

What are the unique features of your work? How did you find your style?

I believe that the main characteristic of my work is creativity. Even when I'm doing fan art, I try to create a new design and not just paint in a different way or in another pose. I like to create new things. I study several styles, like realistic and cartoon. My drawings have mixtures of both styles. By studying several artistic styles, I believe that I have not yet defined my own, but I am not in a hurry to find a style. I prefer to continue studying and never limit my horizons.

How do you gather materials in your daily life and apply them to your work?

Every day I see my social network, and I follow several 2D and 3D artists that I admire. Even when I'm watching a movie or playing a video game, if an interesting character design appears, I try to save the image or sketch anything in my sketchbook, something that reminds me of that design. In my sketchbook I scribble every idea that comes up, and it is where I study several different designs.

1 | 2 3

1
Protoss Assassin

2
Earth Golem 02

3
Earth Golem 03

1
2

1
Onyxia Fanart

2
Fire Elementals 02

1 | 1
Deathwing Fanart

Deathwingall 01

Deathwingall 02

Deathwingall 03

Deathwingall 04

Deathwingall 05

Deathwingall 06

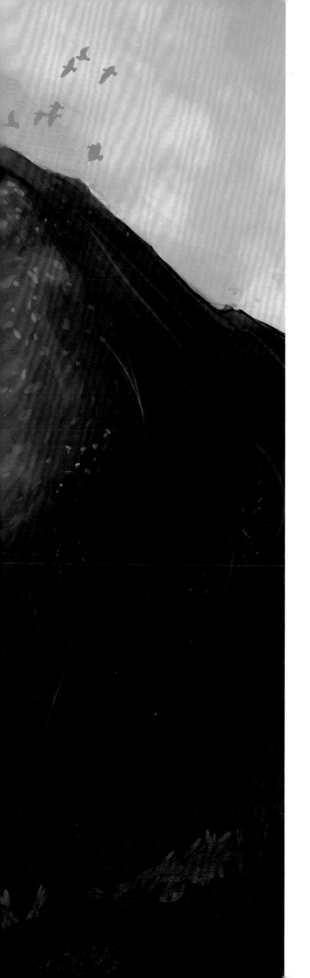

Chapter 2
Traditional Hand Drawing

Ellerie Crum

Materials and tools
Acrylic, Adobe Photoshop
Artist website
www.lcrumart.com

Ellerie (L) is a time-traveling animal trainer who resides in the realm of imagination. She graduated from the Academy of Art University (AAU) with a BFA in illustration and is currently attending graduate studies at Savannah College of Art and Design (SCAD) in Savannah, Georgia. In her spare time, she writes and illustrates stories.

Where do you usually find inspiration for monster design?

I get inspiration from the stories where the creatures inhabit. Creature design is not just about creating awesome designs. It's also about using story and description to bring something entirely new to life.

What tools and materials do you prefer? What are their features and how do they help you with your work?

Basic drawing tools are the most important part of any artist's toolkit. Being able to draft solid drawings is the best foundation for a successful work of art. I work in both acrylic and digital painting, using a Cintiq to break the barrier between digital and traditional areworks in Adobe Photoshop.

1 | 2

1
Nunnehi
Cave-dwelling faeries of the high mountains.

2
Lost in Silence
Robot trapped in ruins.

Do you have a favorite monster design, from either a movie or a game? What inspired you about the design?

My favorite movie monster is H. R. Giger's Alien concept. His work is dark, rich, and terrifying. It has also influenced monster concept art since its creation. I also enjoy the design of Alien's enemy, Predator, as well as various creatures found in the worlds of "Final Fantasy."

How do you gather materials in your daily life and apply them to your work?

Since my work relies on realism, I collect and create many different items to use as references. I visit Renaissance festivals and leather shops to gather animal pelts and skeletons. I also create simple maquettes to use as a reference when lightening difficult compositions.

1 | 2

1
Keelut
Eaters of the dead.

2
Ancient Dragon
Dragon at the edge of the earth.

1
Mishipeshu
Based on native
American myth.

1
Earth Dragon
Elemental dragon.

Tan Zhi Hui

Materials and tools
Adobe Photoshop, Wacom Intuos 5
Artist website
http://www.kudaman-art.com/

Tan Zhi Hui, a passionate concept artist and illustrator who inspires others to be creative. He graduated as a digital animator from The One Academy. He is currently a freelance concept artist and illustrator based in Malacca, Malaysia. Tan provides services such as character design, game splash art, print design, and various illustrations, to the biggest clients in the industry like Capcom, Blizzard Entertainment, Sony Interactive Entertainment and Microsoft Studios.

When did you start designing monsters?

Monsters have always been my favorite things to draw. The reason why I draw a lot of monsters is that it is really fun to explore different designs, forms and elements without limitations! The first time I got to draw a monster professionally was for a game called "Shadow of the Beast." The opportunity was given to me when I worked on the Passion Republic project in 2014. I learned a lot by working on that project.

1	2	3

1
Pokemon Sun and Moon
Pokemon Sun and Moon starters redesign.

2
9C - Team Popplio

3
9A - Team Rowlet

TEAM ROWLET

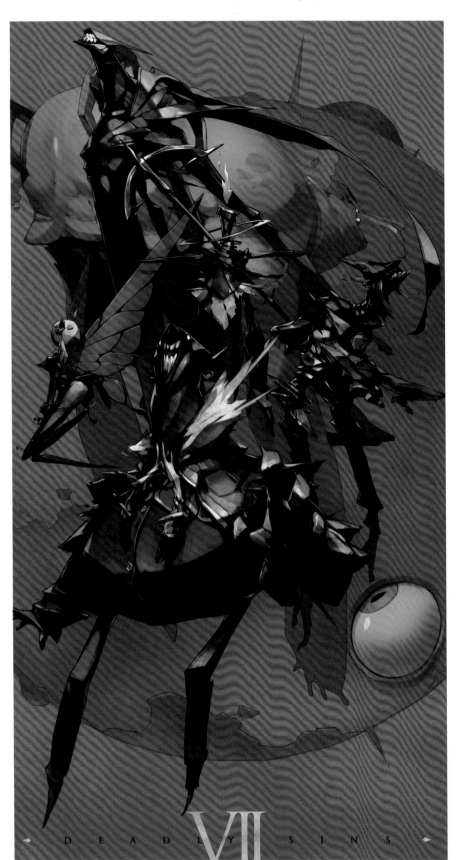

1 2 | 3

1
Seven Deadly Sins
Personel work. I couldn's resist to draw this after watching "Se7en" by David Fincher. It is also a test to see if you have a dirty mind.

2
Heavy Metal
Submission to Character Design Challenge on Facebook. Theme: Heavy Metal. It wasn't easy to make a fat cat that looks like a bad ass. The tattoo on his arm definitely helped.

3
Maori Warrior
Submission to Character Design Challenge on Facebook. Maori was the theme. With such big horns on his head I can't imagine how tiring it can be.

Where do you find inspiration for monster design?

The works of other artists usually are the sources of my inspiration. I look everywhere, record all of the favorite elements and analyze the interesting features and then store them into a database by classification.
Of course, you can make a record of everything you like such as movies, animations and so on. All of those are enough for your reference.

Which artists or art forms have had the biggest influence on you?

I admire artists who have unique and outstanding styles. T-Wei (http://t-wei.tumblr.com/) influenced me the most in terms of the shapes and forms of his characters. He is an amazing artist whose style is second to none.
Sachin Teng (http://www.sachinteng.com/) is another great artist I admire a lot. The colors, designs and subjects of his illustrations are always the best.
Tony Riff (https://tonyriff.com/) also influenced me a lot when I was focusing on T-shirt design a few years back, especially in drawing facial expressions for characters. While there are too many of them for me to name one by one, some other artists that I really like are Jim Murray, Enrique Fernandez, Moby Francke and Ashley Wood.

What are the uniqne features of your work? How do you find your style?

My feature is the sharp sensation to shape and to compose. I spend a long time searching for my own style, but came up empty. And then I managed to draw in the way I feel comfortable. For example, I don't like smooth surfaces, so I make them all "boxed." Finally, my own style came about.

MAORI WARRIOR

SIMIAN WARRIOR

1 | 2

1
Simian Warrior
I drew this on my first public live demo. I was trying to
implement more monkey-related elements into the design but
all I could think of was bananas.

2
Gaebel the Tenth
Personal work. A dead soul is wandering around in space.

SONGSTEALER

1 | 2

1
Songstealer
Another submission to Character Design Challenge on Facebook. The theme was Carnival of Venice. I stole the name from a card in Hearthstone.

2
Yurei
Submission to Character Design Challenge on Facebook. Theme: Centaur. One of the most complicated character design I've worked on.

Aviator 01

Aviator 02

Songstealer 01

Songstealer 02

Songstealer 03

Songstealer 04

Seven Deadly Sins 01

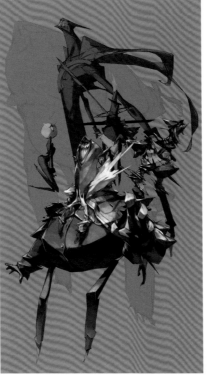
Seven Deadly Sins 02

Seven Deadly Sins 03

Aviator 03

Aviator 04

Metalz 01

Metalz 02

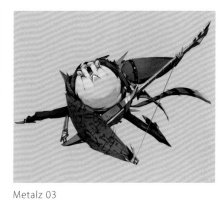

Metalz 03

Yurei 01

Yurei 02

Yurei 03

Maori Warrior 01

Maori Warrior 02

Maori Warrior 03

Alexandre Chaudret

Alexandre Chaudret is a concept artist in the video-game industry and an illustrator. His only goal, every day, is to create and paint freaky monsters and weird universes.

Materials and tools
Adobe Photoshop CC and Wacom Cintiq 13HD
Artist website
http://eyardt.artstation.com/

Where do you usually find inspiration for monster design?

In my opinion, inspiration is everywhere, especially in the case of monsters. Each dark corner of our world is a home for those weird creatures, and I feed off of those fears. I always think of monsters in this context: How can I take something that is so horrible and make it as beautiful as possible? After all, who said that monsters are only bad guys? Whether in books, movies, comics or the internet, the world is an incredible library for any artist who wants to bring monsters to life.

1 | 2

1
Lucius Porcatus
Personal artwork for the greatest boar hero of all time.

2
Charon Obulus
Black Heavy Metal disc cover "Obulus," by Mocking Goliath (2015).

Whether it's from a movie or a video game, which monster design is your favorite and why? How did the design inspire you?

There is one design that I will always keep in mind : Pyramid Head, from the video game "Silent Hill 2." It is the kind of monster that transcends its role to become a legend. Everyone knows Pyramid Head, right? Even if you don't, he at least inspires an instant fear, from his shape to lore and background. He is the personification of the main characters' sin.
In addition, the whole Dark Souls and Bloodborne series (from Software) is just a treasure trove of terrific monsters. It gives me a headache just thinking about trying to figure all of them out.

How do you gather materials in your daily life and apply them to your work?

I simply observe the usual and common things in my life, and feel like I don't fit in. Work, the small problems of everyday life … these are issues that we all have and time passes so fast.

Do you ever feel like if you had the chance to, with a magic key, enter a magic door and leave everything in this world behind? You'd probably take the key and do it.
I sometimes feel that I would do this if I could, with no fears.
The only thing holding me back are my wife and daughter.
But we can all create a new world in our minds, one that fits our aspirations and inspirations. And to create this world, we need the real one .
Do you see how my mind is circling around?

Could you please tell me more about you work? How did you find your style?

A friend of mine told me once, "If there are red clothes, exposed guts and at least one skull, no doubt it's one of Alex's works." I confess! This is correct. I like to create, and by that I mean having fun in all the ways possible while painting or drawing. I like to create strong vibrations through colors and composition, sometimes focusing on the most precise details or simply tasting the energy of rough brush strokes.

1   2 | 3

1
The Amazon
Personal artwork
for a dark fantasy
project, full of
bones and skulls.

2
The Happy Chopper
"Choppy, chopp'
chopp'
Here comes the
Happy Chopper
Choppy chopp'
chopp'
Keep your head down
Here comes the
Happy Chopper... "

3
The Countess
Personal artwork
for a fantasy
universe, full of
bones and skulls
(and
vampires…).

1
Ash Storm
Personal artwork for a
fantasy universe, based
on anciant forgotten
gods.

2
Hell Silent Screamer
Personal artwork for a
fantasy universe, based
on anciant forgotten
gods.

Anti Matter

Materials and tools
Needle Pen, Brush, Mark Pen, Watercolor, Color Lead and Propylene
Artist website
www.antimatterzxl.com

Anti Matter majored in animation at the Facwlty of Distarce and continued Education of the Communication University of China in Shanghai. After graduation, he participated in a project about films and games. He is good at hand drawing, and his works are full of imagination. He likes movies, painting and walking around.

Where do you find inspiration for designing monsters?

I get some of my inspiration from the biological world, some from dreams and also some from what I hear and see. The design of monsters is not always based on the biological world. Sometimes a small object in your life can be a source of inspiration. Multi-species, cross-racial rational splicing is also essential. My inspiration comes from the association and deformation of seemingly unrelated things.

1 | 2

1
Lizard
This lizard has a crocodile-like tail. It has five pairs of eyes which can see in multiple directions at the same time. The lizard is a meat-eater and tackles its prey like a lion. When in danger, it can spray paralytic smog from the protuberance on either side of its back.

2
Skull Monster
Its skeleton is exposed and looks like an animal skull. Its size is similar to a chimpanzee; likewise, it runs with its feet. It has a sensitive sense of smell. The creature's tail is a destructive weapon, and its claw is capable of dishing out fatal blows.

What tools and materials do you prefer? What are their features and how do they help you with your work?

I like to use tools such as a needle pen, a brush, a mark pen, watercolor, color lead and propylene. The strokes of the needle are clear and smooth, so it is my first choice for drawing lines. When creating a draft a brush is also a very good choice. Mark's color is saturated and has a gradient effect, but after drying it will become lighter. Watercolor is a good material to improve the richness of pictures. The color is uncertain, and it always brings unexpected effects. I often use color pencil drawings to determine a general color scheme, because it's easy to cover, and it helps boldly explore the color direction. I usually use acrylics to emphasize some bright and prominent colors and positions, to increase the levels in the painting.

As a concept artist, could you share some of your important experiences?

Don't solidify your mind. The source of inspiration can be diversified. It's important to watch life and nature around you. Design should be reasonable, but don't be limited and bound by it. There are many incredible creatures in nature. Their physical qualities are often beyond your imagination, so don't be afraid to experiment. A lot of people around you will make some suggestions or question your work. You should learn how to screen this information. If you're going be the master of your own work, other people's suggestions and questions are not always going to be beneficial. Use your own judgement and be persistent.

1

2

Fish Monster

Fish Monster is the product of radiation experiments in the laboratory. Gene mutations made this creature huge and caused its limbs to evolve. Because of the increase in brain capacity, its intelligence is equivalent to that of a 5-year-old child. Although its appearance is frightening, it is gentle and curious about the outside world.

How do you gather materials in your daily life and apply them to your works?

I browse websites, collect pictures, and record some interesting things with my mobile phone when I go out. These materials are not necessarily related to the design, but can be useful in the creation and drafting stage. In order to make the details look more realistic, I will select the skin texture of real animals to use as a reference.

1	2
	3

1
Insectchicken
Insectchicken is a carnivorous animal. It looks like a chicken, but it has a worm head, so it's named insectchicken. It resembles a turkey and attacks its prey with a sickle-shaped tentacle on its back. Its mouth secretes a digestive saliva that liquifies the flesh of prey. Because it doesn't have eyes, it relies on ultrasound waves to avoid obstacles and chase prey.

2
Plant Spirit
This monster is part animal/part plant. The crown of the creature has a coronary plant that produces irritating pollen. When exposed to it, other organisms become allergic or comatose. The Plant Spirit's mouth is located on its back, where it can snatch small mammals and insects. When food is scarce, it relies on water and photosynthesis to reduce body metabolism and survive for a long period of time.

3
Sonic Dragon
Its head can send infrasonic waves to attack the enemy. It relies on sound waves to get around. It can damage vital organs by adjusting the vibration frequency. The Sonic Dragon is an omnivorous creature.

1

1
Multipedworm
Multipedworm is an omnivorous animal. It's a large animal, with an adult body length of up to eight meters, and lives in swamp or deep forest. It has mucus on the surface of its body and glands in its mouth that secrete toxic venom and strong corrosive saliva.

1 | 3
2 |

1

Three-eye Pterosaur

Its eyes are like those of a chameleon and can rotate to observe things nearby. It flies through air with ease and consumes insects, bats, and small birds. Its nest is located inside a rock cave.

2

The Mask

It looks cute and adorable, but is actually really fierce and brutal. It often confuses its prey with a silly guise, and opens its mouth when its prey relaxes its vigilance. The glands in its mouth secrete neurotoxins. Its vitality is tenacious and it can only be killed by internal injuries.

3

The Three-tailed Monster

This lizard has 10 limbs. Claws protrude from the end of its three tails. The creature uses its forelimbs to control its prey, with one of the tails dedicated to sucking liquid from its victims. Its two huge arms are capable of ripping apart bodies. The thee-tailed Monster has gills on both sides of its head, which allow them to live in water.

Gilberto Guadalupe Sánchez Reyes

Materials and tools
Pencils, Watercoolor, Acrylic, Paper, Paint, Ink, Brushes, Spray and Aerofrafo.
Artist website
https://www.behance.net/ilustraciongg

Gilberto G. Sánchez Reyes, a.k.a. "Krotalon" is an illustrator, designer and restorer of art. Gilberto likes to recreate fantastic characters and environments. He was born in Mexico City and lives in Ciudad Nezahualcóyotl, where he used to draw creatures and monsters since he was little. Gilberto studied design and visual communication. He has worked as an art director in advertising agencies and for the National Institute of Fine Arts, as mural restoration officer. His works have been published in different international posters, illustrations and stickers.

Which artists or art forms have had the biggest influence on you?

Gerald Brom, RK Post, Daren Bader and Robert Bliss are the main artists who have influenced my work. I admire their great creativity and ingenuity to create monsters and fantastic characters.

Chapter 2: Traditional Hand Drawing

1 | 2

1
Monstruo del Pantano

2
Black Demon

What tools and materials do you prefer? What are their features and how do they help you with your work?

I prefer to use pencil and paper to sketch and to execute a work. Traditional techniques like watercolor, acrylic and ink are my favorite. I like the result of painting on wood, as its durability helps to preserve the work for a longer period of time. With a digital project, I feel comfortable using a tablet and any special software to illustrate.

As a concept artist, could you share some of your important experiences?

I participated in a manga drawing competition, organized by the Embassy of Japan, where I competed with other artists from different states. I won the first place by drawing a samurai demon with a pencil.

Either from a movie or a game, what's your favorite monster design?

Definitely my favorite monster is from the movie "Alien" from 1979. I like its humanoid form – acid instead of blood – and the way it attacks its victims.

1	2	
3	4	5

1
Gnomo

2
Ghorn

3
ORC

4
General de Guerra Orko

5
Ilus

Peter Jude Rocque

Materials and tools
Adobe Photoshop, Pencil on Paper
Artist website
https://peterrocque.artstation.com/

Based in Bangalore, India, as a 2D concept artist and digital illustrator, Peter has worked on creating character illustrations, stylized characters designs and background concepts for social games in the art services department of a gaming studio. Over the course of his career, he had an inclination towards designing villainous characters or monsters as they allow him to push a certain level of detail that compliments their persona more than others.

Where do you usually find inspiration for monster design?

Creating monsters is especially interesting as you have to visualize something that does not exist. It's challenging to come up with a story behind the creature, which helps me with the design. I usually base my designs on a central concept: an animal or some elements and functions that I would like to see in the character. I then slowly build up a back story that makes it all come together. The inspiration for me would be an idea that just clicks, and you want to best describe it pictorially.

1 | 2

1
Monster Concept
Born and raised in the underbelly of the infernal realm; answering only to his superiors, he is equipped and battle-ready to bring any foe to their knees. Those who refuse him will be devoured, resting as imprisoned souls within his body.

2
Sympathy for the Devil
The Prince of Darkness sits with pride on his throne, immersed in his cynical and diabolical plans for self-glory and the uprise of his kingdom to come.

What artists or art forms have most influenced your work?

I have been fascinated by the works by Joe Madureira, Jerad Marantz and Patrick Brown. These three are among my greatest influences. I used to love comic book characters and would constantly draw them growing up. I especially love the artwork from the video game "Darksiders". After playing it, I began doing a lot of works that were inspired by the style of the game.

What are the unique features of your work? How did you find your style?

Like any person, we all have our likes and dislikes. We find certain elements that appeal to us the most. We also interpret information differently from each other. That's how we cultivate our own style. It's the way we process information and reflect it on our work. It could be either details or just different techniques. I like glossy materials, mean-looking expressions, organic surfaces with an edgy and flowy design. These elements essentially define my style. It takes time to find your style. The more we observe and learn, the more we can add to our work.

1 | 2

1
Do you want a balloon?
Any child's birthday nightmare would have an evil clown on a murderous rampage, who lures you by offering balloons, candy and such. Especially on a day like Halloween.

2
Can I play with Madness?
To ward off unwanted trespassers, this scarecrow has stealth tactics and convenient surroundings. Anyone who crosses him would meet their inevitable fate, much like what his right hook suggests.

How do you gather materials in your daily life and apply them to your work?

I always have a main idea or key feature that I design my characters around. Step two would be imagining other elements that would work well to enhance its appeal. I watch a lot of movies, play video games and read. This sort of thing becomes a visual library stored away in your head to draw upon when you work. In general, I am observant of my surroundings, and you can often stumble upon very interesting things found in and around you that could be useful while creating designs.

1 | 2

1
Bad to the Bone
Themed around a fascination for Halloween. He wanted to create his own version of characters based on the festivity.

2
Zombie
This one used to be a homeless person, now turned to a zombie. The cause for his mutation also left him disfigured and made him pale and blue skinned.

Cicman

Materials and tools
Wacom, Propelling Pencil, Watercolor
Artist website
http://www.zcool.com. cn/u/13740773

As a student at Lu Xun Academy of Fine Arts, an art school in Liaoning, China, in the Department of Animation Design, Cicman is very interested in concept design. He is also interested in the subject of traditional Chinese mythology.

When did you start designing monsters?

From the time I was a child, I always liked to draw. I first got an idea about the prototype from the internet when studying at university and immediately fell in love with it. I later spent about one year exploring this area and finally chose monster design.

What tools and materials do you prefer? What are their features and how do they help you with your work?

Since childhood, I've always enjoyed drawing illustrations and cartoons, and I continue to do it even though I've moved on to CG painting. I have two notebooks: one for practice and the other for sketching outlines. After that, I can color them on computer.

1
Shahe Monster
This is the image of the Shahe monster. He was addicted to killing. The monster made life for the Liushahe a hell on earth. The nine-skull head on his chest consists of nine heads of the sutra-seeker.

2
Ghost Warrior Jiula
In the chaotic medieval times, the order of society collapsed. The ghost warrior appeared during this period, and he was a disorderly supporter.

1

The Battle of the Porcine Demon

In this story, the monkey king is on a journey to the West to catch the porcine demon. The pig monster, originally a marshal of the world, was later derogated into a mortal and turned into a bloodthirsty pig demon.

1

The Golden Winged Monster

Named Peng, the golden winged monster is the biggest bird in the legend. People in the city were nearly eaten by him.

2

Ginseng Tree

This treefolk is nourished by human blood. Through this process it is able to shape into the fruit of the children.

1

1
Yuhua State
The Nine Spirit Yuan Saint is a demon that does not eat human food. The picture depicts a scene of him fighting with the monkey king's brother.

1

1
The Devil
This painting shows the
demon king. He has a
bloody mouth, iron bronze
teeth, a huge roar, and
mighty glory. He is a
murderous fiend that takes
a human shape.

Where do you usually find inspiration for monster design?

I love horror movies as well as horror games. I also like going to the zoo to find inspiration.

How do you gather materials in your daily life and apply them to your works?

When I just started drawing monsters, I always browsed the internet to collect a variety of materials in my spare time. But I seldom reviewed them. I currently like exploring on my own. What you see with your own eyes is something different from the pictures on the internet. Also, I like going to bookstores to look at some interesting photo albums.

1

1
Silver Horns
This is the page boy of Lord Lao Zi. He stole the Magic Gourd of Lord Lao Zi and came to earth as the incarnation of silver king. He absorbed the soul through various instruments.

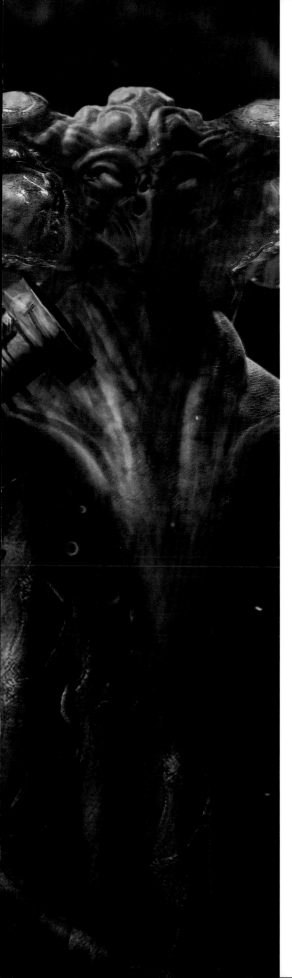

Chapter 3
3D Modeling & Rendering

Fredo Viktor Bernardo

Materials and tools
*Zbrush, Substance Painter, Maya,
Octane Render, KeyShot,
Photoshop*
Artist website
http://www.fredoartviktor.com/

1 | 2

1
Vampire Beast 01

2
Vampire Beast 02

3
Vampire Beast 03

As a 3D digital artist, most of Fredo's works center on characters and creatures for various projects like TV or films. As of this writing, most of his projects are for the gaming and 3-D printing industries. At the heart of his artist profession, his real love is learning new methods and techniques, as well as doing research on the concepts and components of the project he is going to create.

Monster design is a highly imaginative work. Where do you usually find inspiration?

Nature mostly and ordinary things around me. I just copy from life, the real stuff.

Which artists or art forms have most influenced your style?

There are a lot of great artists out there whom I look up to, but if I have to pick my top two it would be Bernini and Caravaggio. Almost all their artworks, paintings and sculptures have awakened the artist in me. Seeing their works and learning about their life stories have kept me going through those times when I felt very uncertain whether I should continue to be an artist or not. Every time I do any art, whether monsters, fantasies or realistic human figures, I try very hard to bring my work a tiny step closer to their masterful creations.

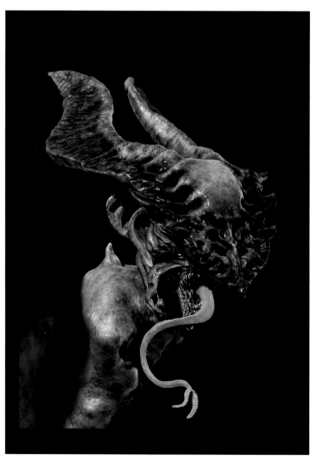

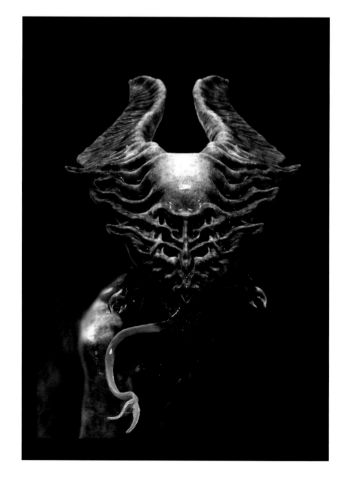

What tools and materials do you prefer? What are their features and how do they help you with your work?

In Zbrush, just the basic brushes like standard, dam standard, move and clay brushes help me a lot in getting all my sculpting work done. Zmodeler and Zspheres help me to block out models fast or create a nice base mesh to sculpt on. And when I need to do fine-tuning or am just unsure of which course to take in my sculpting and need to test ideas first, the layers function provides me with that non-destructive workflow I need.

What are the features of your work? How do you find your style?

I don't think I have a particular style; I believe my artwork will continuously evolve as I continue to learn and explore. But when I get commissioned to do a certain style or I want to do a personal project on a subject I got interested in, I do a lot of research, study and preliminary art tests first about the kind of art style the project requires. In that way, I can adapt to the art project and be the artist who gives life to it.

1 2 | 3

1
Part of Serpent God

2
Details of Serpent God

3
Serpent God

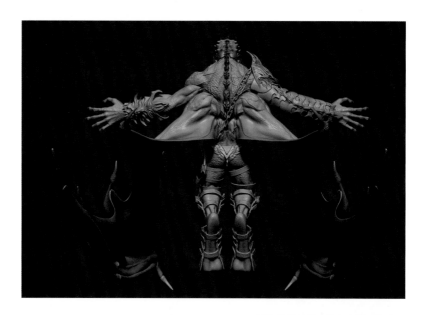

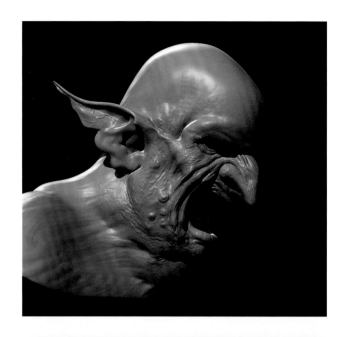

1
1920s Vamp Wip B

2
1920s Vamp BW

3
1920s Vampire Clay

4
1920s Vamp Colored

Jan Löchler

Materials and tools
ZBrush, Photoshop, KeyShot
Artist website
www.behance.net/3D-Ghost

Jan is originally a graphic designer working for an advertising agency. He was always interested in the technologies behind video games and VFX in movies. Finally he started doing 3D design about six years ago. Jan likes the studies of species and anatomies as much as he likes the sculpting process. The journey from a rough idea to the result fascinates him ever since. Jan enjoys the opportunity to animate a model or create a 3D print and bring it to life. Jan likes to mix up different genres, picking and choosing which styles and details he likes from each and orienting his own designs accordingly. The process is very free and different each time. Sometimes the design changes dramatically during the process, but that's the fun part which opens new worlds.

When did you start designing monsters?

I started creating fantasy creatures in 2011. I've been a big fan of VFX movies and games ever since I was a child, and I always wanted to do my own stuff.

1 | 2

1
Gray Dragon

2
Dragon RGB

Monster design is a highly imaginative work. Where do you find inspiration?

I get my inspiration from different sources. Sometimes I like to redesign creatures I see somewhere (in a movie or game), or I start from a real existing animal and combine it with other elements from nature or my imagination to create something new (for example, a lizard was the starting point for the dragon design).

What tools and materials do you prefer? What are their features and how do they help you with your work?

I like to work with ZBrush from the beginning till the end of the project. It's very fast to make a base to start, and you're able to change the shape of the model very quickly and try something new.

As a concept artist, could you share some of your important experiences?

You should like what you do. If I would like to have the creature as a statue on my desk, I know I'm on the right way. Often it helps if you have a little story around the character to make the image more interesting for the viewer. With 3D works, it especially helps if you have a finished model that you can easily duplicate and slightly change the pose or accessories to create a scene instead of just a single character (for example, an Oger).

| 1 | 2 | 1 |

1
Oger in Black and White

2
Oger with Colors

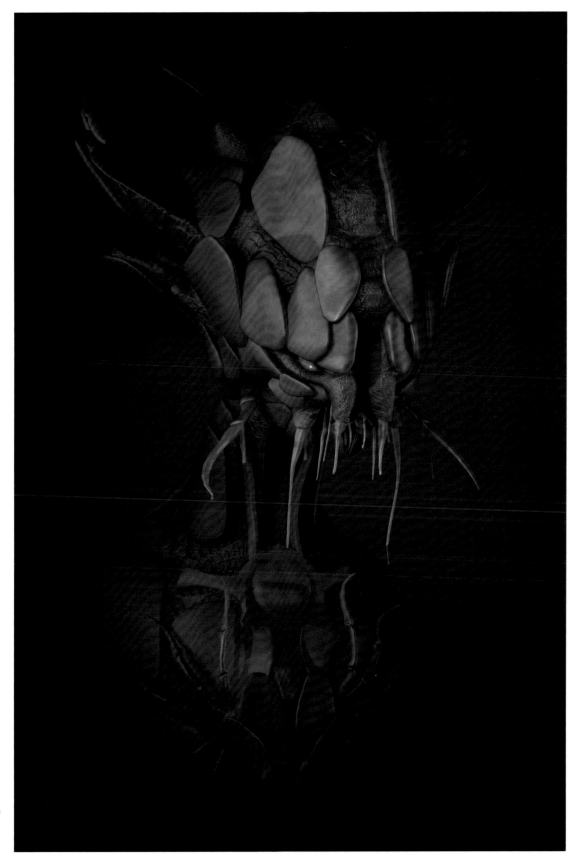

1

Process of Beast

2

Process of Mechknight

3

Process of Dragon

4

Process of Mechsuit

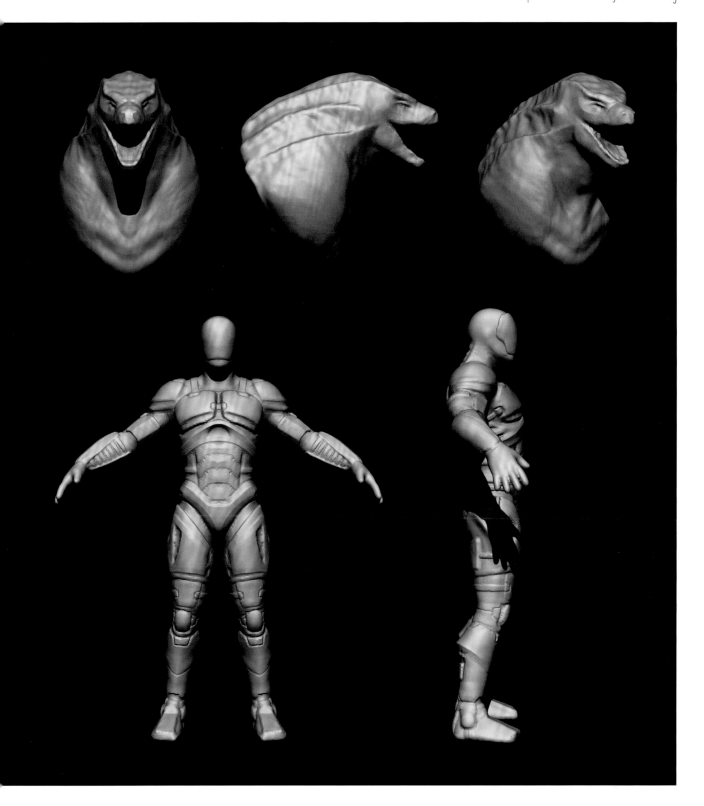

Arturo Ramirez Acosta

Materials and tools
ZBrush, Maya, KeyShot, Substance Painter and Photoshop
Artist website
https://www.artstation.com/ artist/limkuk

As a digital graphic designer and lover of special effects, Arturo is the director and founder of Underkraken Studio, which specializes in 3D.

When did you start designing monsters?

I began three years ago after I graduated from university.
I've always enjoyed creating characters.

Monster design is a highly imaginative work. Where do you usually find inspiration?

As a concept artist, it's very important to study a lot of animal and human anatomy. Artists should also watch closely the details in nature, in animals, insects and flowers.

La única verdad que conocemos es la mentira...

1	2
1 Liar	2 Hungry

W A R T O R T L E
THE FIGHTER

C A R N A G E

AZRAEL BATMAN

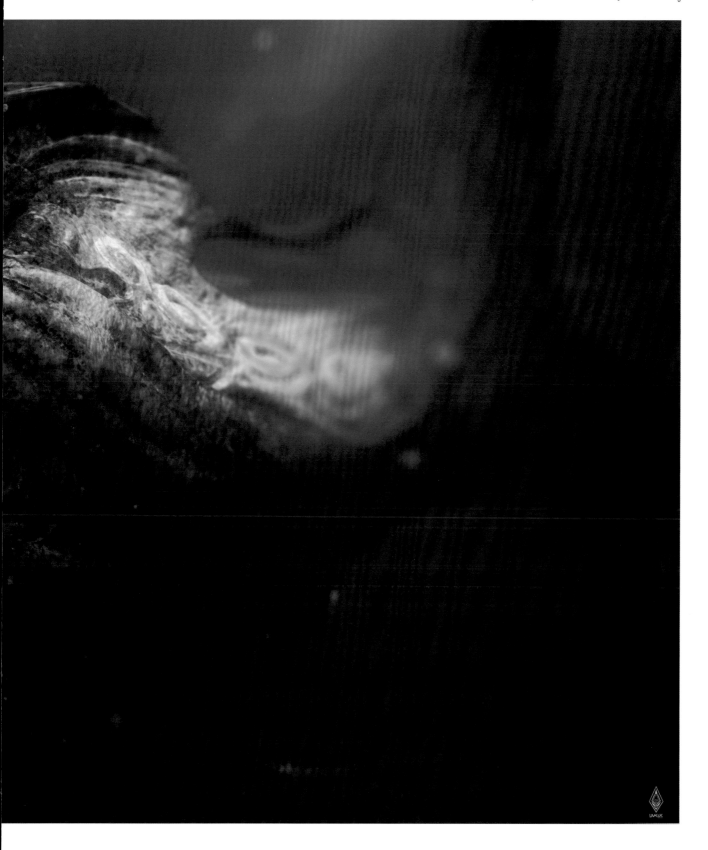

Which artist or art forms have influenced you the most?

I admire four artists in the world: Alex Alvarez from Gnomon, Rafael Grassetti, Dominic Qwek and Kurt Papstein. The way they create characters, creatures and new concepts is what makes me follow their work.

What are the unique features of your work? How do you find your style?

I think what stands out about my work is my color of palettes. I usually use cold colors and occasionally some pinks, reds and oranges. The lighting is also another factor. I really like dramatic lighting.

1
Metal Slug - Mars People

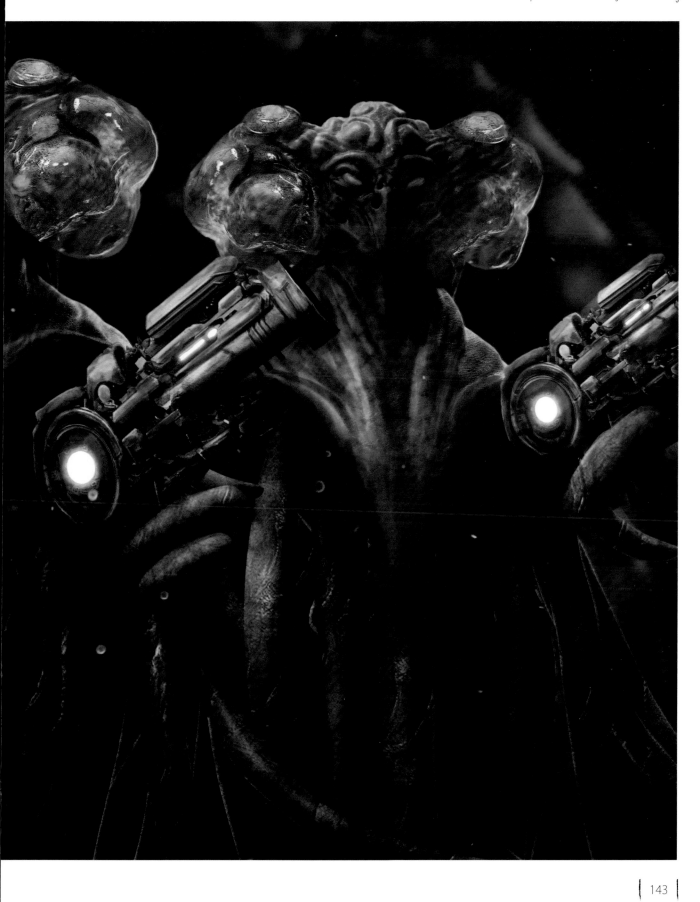

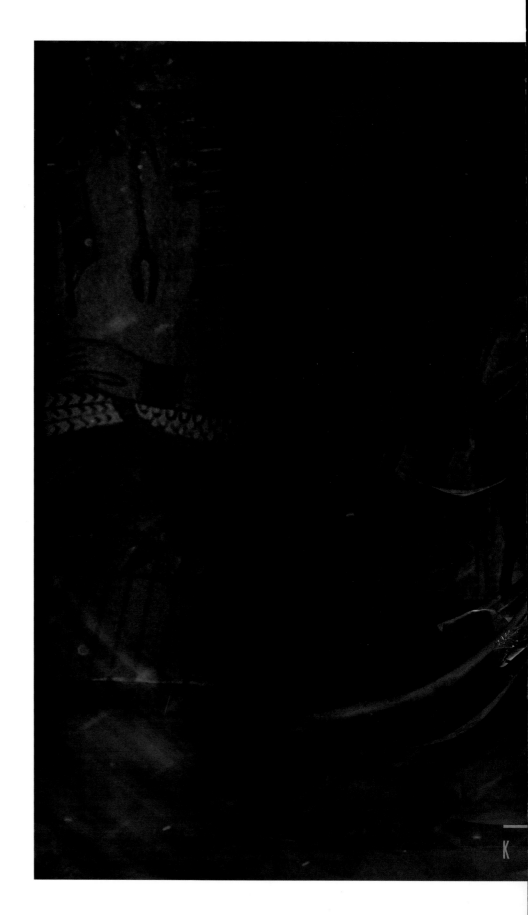

POWER RANGERS
G SPHINX

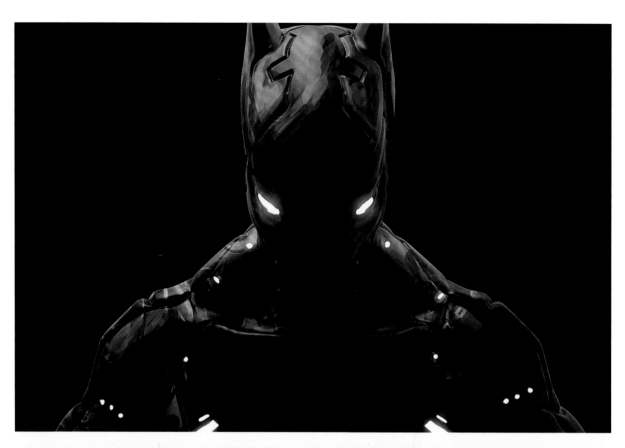

1 | 3
2 |

1
Batman Beyond
Exploration 01

2
Sponge Bob/Cockroach

3
Batman Beyond
Exploration 02

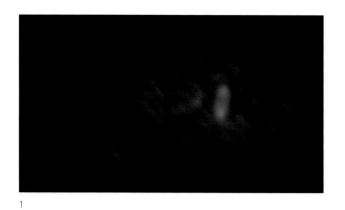

1

2

3

4

5

6

7

8

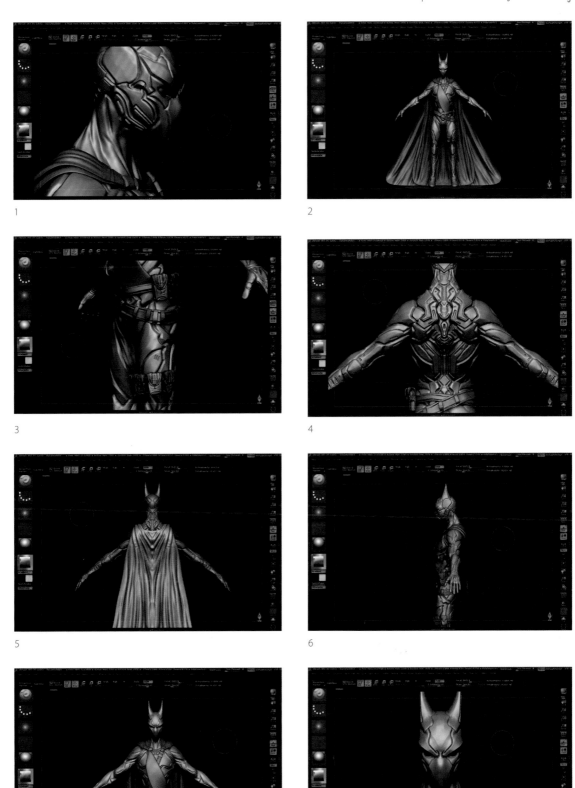

1

2

3

4

5

6

7

8

Marco Hasmann

Materials and tools
Mainly Good ol' Pencil, Zbrush, Photoshop, and Substance Painter/Designer; Rendering usually goes to KeyShot for Offline Rendering, and Marmoset Toolbag 2 for Real-Time assets.

Artist website
https://www.artstation.com/artist/hasmann
http://hasmann.weebly.com/

Marco is a freelance illustrator and concept artist specializing in horror, sci-fi and fantasy themes in both 2D and 3D environments.

When did you start designing monsters?

I started creating monsters at an early age; like most of the kids I had a vivid imagination and an eye for critters and horrific monsters. It started becoming a kind of work in my 20s when I created my first album cover for my metal band's first release.

Monster design is a highly imaginative job. Where do you usualfy find inspiration?

Nature, mostly. There's some crazy-looking insects and sea creatures out there that can blow your mind away. Movies and video games also play an important role as it's always good to check other artists' works to motivate yourself and improve.

1	2

1
Celatid Alien, XCom 2 Mod

2
Devouring the Infinity

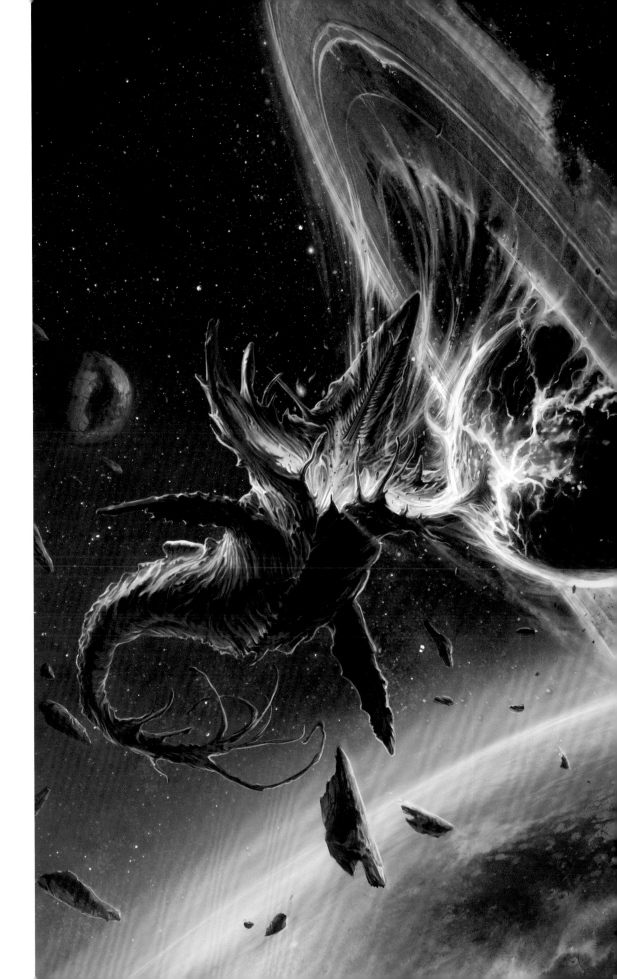

Which artists or art forms have had the biggest influence on you?

Paul Bonner, Zdzislaw Beksinski, H • R • Giger are my main influences; as a kid I grew up with a lot of Warhammer references and inspirations, mainly from the works by Ian Miller and later on Adrian Smith's illustrations.

What tools and materials do you prefer? What are their features and how do they help you with your work?

I always start doing some little sketches and silhouettes with just a pencil, laying down some very crude ideas and shapes. It's way faster for me to start with a general idea of what I'm going to do before approaching the software; when working for illustrations I still like sketching the main element with pencils and later port them in Photoshop for final adjustments and changes. I use mainly Photoshop for 2D illustrations and concepts; 3D works are usually approached in ZBrush where I can move big shapes quickly. Then if it's for real-time usage (video games), I texture in Substance Painter and check out the final results in Marmoset; for 3D concepts I mainly use Polypaint directly in Zbrush and render it with KeyShot. The final adjustments are always done in Photoshop.

It's the final sketch after going through some changes on the main creature; it's better to have a fairly clear idea of where the design is heading before approaching the coloring/ painting phase.

I always prefer working directly with colors instead of detailing first with just black and white values, so laying down an initial palette is crucial to me.

The final illustration: it's always worth to give final adjustments to contrast and color saturation.

1 | 1
The Rendering Process

The base pencil sketch, after some repositioning in Photoshop.

As always, I lay down the initial palette first and the base values for the whole image.

The almost completed piece has most of the detailing done, just need a little more push.

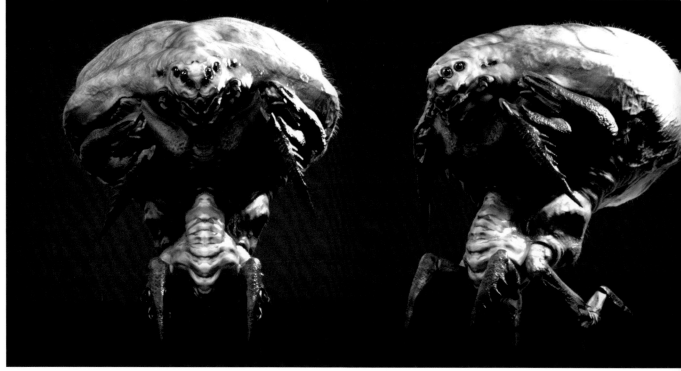

1   2   3

Viperbug   Viperbug Turnaround   Viperbug Pose

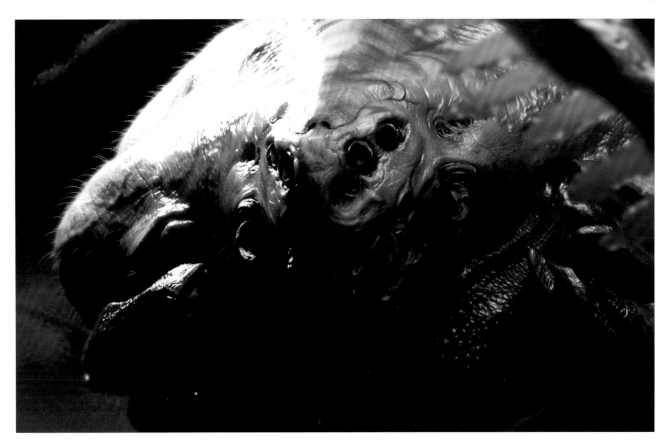

Chapter 4
Sculpture

Jin Hao Villa

Materials and tools
Zbrush, KeyShot, Maya Photoshop
Artist website
http://villadome-cg.com

Based in Manila, Philippines, Jin is 33 years old. He has worked as a digital sculptor, character artist, character designer and 3D illustration designer for video games, film/animation and 3D printing in recent years.

When did you start designing monsters?

I started creating monster designs back in 2005 when Zbrush was still in its second version. The software really gave me the opportunity to be creative. Then shortly after, 3D was starting to be used for concept designers, hence came the title "3D concept designer." I started extending my service to freelance work, and in 2014, I finally began receiving character design requests from clients.

Monster design is a highly imaginative Job. Where do you usually find inspiration for?

I get my inspiration from my favorite artists, and the video games/films I grew up with.

1 | 2

1
Traditional Toad Clay Sculpture in 3D

2
Thanatos Tyrant 03

Which artists or art forms have influenced you the most?

Artists such as Kris Costa, Gio Nakpil, Carlos Huante, H • R • Giger and Jerad Marantz have influenced much of my style.

What tools and materials do you prefer? What are their features and how do they help you with your work?

Zbrush is my main choice for sculpting, KeyShot for rendering, Maya for basic 3D modeling, and Photoshop for completing work.

As a concept artist, could you share some of your important experiences?

I would start off understanding basic principles for design like silhouette, shape, gesture, rhythm, unity and contrast. Then I'd go and make a sketch in 2D of multiple thumbnails and line art for character designs that best represent what I am trying to go for.

Keita Okada

Materials and tools
ZBrush, KeyShot, Photoshop
Artist website
https://yuzuki.artstation.com/

Keita was born in July 4, 1991. He became a freelance artist in 2015, and has been a successful modeler working on mainly creature modeling that includes the big title "Bloodborne." Keita has won several awards such as ZBrush Central Top Row Award and 3DTotal Excellent Award, and he has been featured in popular CG magazines. Keita established a digital sculpting company, Villard Inc., in 2017.

When did you start designing monsters?

I've always loved drawing dragons and monsters since I was little. I decided to be a creature artist while I was in high school, and I entered into this business. H • R • Giger has hugely influenced me too.

Monster design is a highly imaginative work. Where do you usually find inspiration?

I regularly watch movies that feature creatures, and I get my inspiration from that. Art communities like Art Station also inspire me a lot.

1 | 2

1
ZBrush Document

2
People of Variant

What tools and materials do you prefer? What are their features and how do they help you with your work?

I love using ZBrush and KeyShot. Those tools allow me to create varieties of ideas and designs into 3D efficiently. Using ZBrush requires you to have a high drawing skill since the program is for sculpting, but KeyShot lets you make high-quality rendered images easily.

What are the unique features of your work? How do you find your style?

People always mention about how dynamic my creations are. I always put a focus on movements to make models more dynamic, and I say that's the main feature of my art. I have found the style through speed sculpting.

1
2   3

1
Giraffe (kirin)

2
Dragon Concept

3
Creature Concept Model

Creature Concept

1 | 3
2 | 4

1
Baku

2
Turblent Lion

3
Heavy Dragon

4
Lion

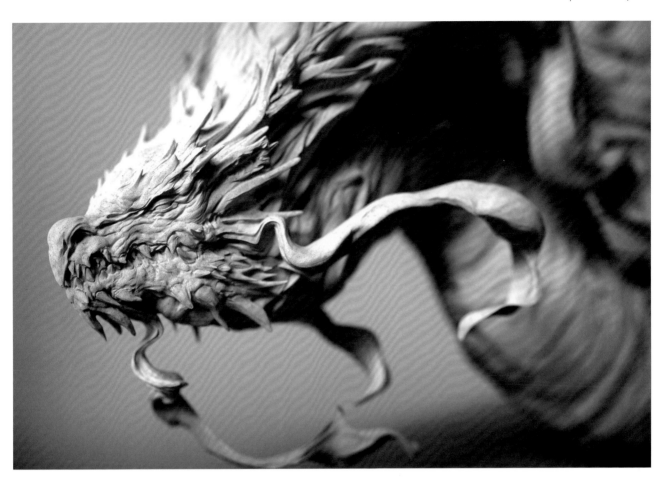

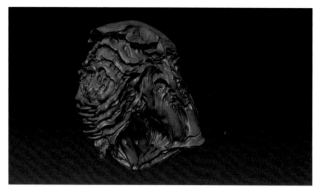

Step 01

Step 02

Step 03

Step 04

Step 05

Step 06

Step 07

Step 08

Step 09

Step 10

Step 11

Step 12

Step 13

Step 14

Step 15

Final

Midas

Materials and tools
Super Sculpey Firm, NSP
Artist website
http://weibo.com/midastouch84

Midas, who graduated from the Fine Arts department of Shanghai Normal University, is a cutting-edge prototype designer in China. He now creates prototypes for games. After some difficulties in the realm of video games, he turned to prototype sculpture. His works are usually based on real monsters and characters in ancient Chinese mythology.

When did you start designing monsters?

I saw some prototypes by designers from the United States and Japan about 10 years ago on the internet and was fascinated by their design creativity. That was when I began to design monsters.

Monster design is a highly imaginative job. Where do you usually find inspiration?

Nature is an amazing designer, and no work can be created without a prototype. Almost all of the designs are based on nature, being reshaped or deformed. From this point, all of my works are inspired by nature.

1
The Side of Ghost Oni

2
The Front of Ghost Oni

Which artists or art forms have influenced you the most?

Takeya Takayuki (Japan) and Mark Newman (the United States) are the two prototype designers I like the most.

What tools and materials do you prefer? What are their features and how do they help you with your work?

I mainly use Super Sculpey Firm when creating prototype sculptures. It has a specific character – you can make a shape, to be heated in the oven, and the form is fixed when cooling down. In this way, you can keep the form you like or reshape it

As a concept artist, could you share some of your important experiences?

I prefer to take notes of what inspires me, whether it is just a word, a picture or a sketch. When I get an idea, I always write it down.

What are the unique features of your work? How do you find your style?

Often the work mirrors the designer's inner world, thus you don't have to find a style. A designer just needs to do what he wants to express himself; the style is a reflection of personality.

How do you gather materials in your daily life and apply them to your works?

Most designers are capable of gathering materials, but many just leave them there It's very important to classify and review the material. I always draw inspiration from reviewing the materials stored in my database.

Monsters of the Imagination:
Amazing Creature Designs by Global Artists

Author: Dopress Books
Commissioning Editors: Guo Guang, Zeng Sheng
English Editors: Jenny Qiu, Xu Xu
Copy Editor: Jimmy Nesbitt
Book Designer: Qiu Hong

First published in the United Kingdom in 2018 by CYPI PRESS

Add: 79 College Road, Harrow Middlesex, HA1 1BD, UK
Tel: +44 (0) 20 3178 7279
E-mail: sales@cypi.net editor@cypi.net
Website: www.cypi.net
ISBN: 978-1-908175-81-6
Printed in China